FERRER-DALMAU

ART, HISTORY, AND MINIATURES

We extend our thanks to the miniaturists reviewed in this book for providing their works for photographic reproduction of the present edition.

Photographers of the miniatures:

Francisco Javier Ruiz González, Jesús Gamarra López, José Francisco Gallardo Porras, Luis Miguel Esteban Laguardia, Miguel Angel Díaz Galeote, and Miguel Angel Pérez Rubio.

Translated from the Spanish by Jonee Tiedemann
Originally published as Ferrer-Dalmau: Arte, historia y miniatura *by Angelma, Spain © September 2012*

FERRER-DALMAU

ART, HISTORY, AND MINIATURES

José Manuel Guerrero Acosta
Agustín Pacheco Fernández
Luis Miguel Esteban Laguardia

with the collaboration of
Miguél Angel Pérez Rubio

Schiffer Publishing Ltd

4880 Lower Valley Road • Atglen, PA 19310

Foreword

The mission of the Institute for Military Culture and History is to protect, conserve, investigate, and diffuse the rich heritage of the Spanish army; this task is consistently realized with the creation of archives, libraries, and museums.

The military museums offer a service open to the public and serve society and its development; they collect a group of cultural patrimony that helps recall Spain's historic military past, which is always a part of Spain´s history and is certainly a burden Spaniards face in an always uncertain future.

In addition to conserving, documenting, and studying historic items they are exhibited with a didactic purpose, disseminating knowledge and familiarity for investigative purposes, education, studies, or mere contemplation; they form spaces that encourage cultural and scientific participation. As such, the Institute strives to gather, support, and organize initiatives such as the one presented here.

This book deals with an exhibit of historic paintings created by Spain's most distinguished painter of contemporary military scenes; his recreations as miniatures are the work of a sizable group of artists who dedicated their time to this creative expression in an altruistic manner. A long and productive artistic tradition is continued here that has set standards and roots in the now very remote nineteenth century.

I would like to thank everyone involved—persons and institutions—who have made this exhibition possible. We want to express our deepest thanks, gratitude, and recognition to the protagonists of historic military activities by presenting them to a Spanish and international audience within the incomparable setting of the Army Museum in the Citadel of Toledo (*Museo del Ejército en el Alcázar de Toledo*).

Madrid, July 2, 2012

Francisco Ramos Oliver

Major General (*General de División*)

Director of the Institute for Military History
and Culture (*Instituto de Historia y Cultura Militar*)

Preface

Among the many artistic expressions that show us the history and traditions of the Spanish army, one of the most notable is without a doubt the historical painting. The Army Museum owns a large number of paintings of this genre, particularly portraits of outstanding military figures represented in various epochs by a voluminous cast of Spanish and international artists.

Our museum also features a large exhibit of military history paintings, which we strive to continuously improve with respect to conservation and where we intend to incorporate new pieces. For this purpose we rely on the recently created Army Museum Foundation, and we hope it will be an important factor. With its collaboration the Institute may pursue an effective schedule for exhibits and the expansion and improvement of its permanent collection, and hence the Spanish army's patrimony—one of the missions of the Institute for Military History and Culture. This will allow us to disseminate this very material culture via its own exhibits, as well as other sources in a fitting setting and within historic context.

Military miniatures have always been an integral part of the museum's collections. We have a special hall where a permanent exhibit features our notable and cherished collection.

It is with great pleasure that we include an exhibit of canvases by noted painter Augusto Ferrer Dalmau, who has accumulated a sizable collection of scenes of Spain's military past. His paintings exude his passion for Spain's history, as well as respect and affection for our companions in arms' image, whether in peacetime or in battle.

This satisfaction is even greater because we are able to present them publicly, accompanied by magnificent recreation with miniatures. These miniatures provide a new dimension to the pictorial work and were created by the most outstanding miniaturists and painters of Spanish figures of our time. They are the best on the international scene, as there are many Spaniards who are very successful with their miniatures at world contests and fairs. They command high prices today within the collector's market and can appropriately be characterized as pieces of art.

I wish to extend my gratitude to the curator of the exhibit, to the artist, and to the miniaturists and their contribution to our museum, which wants to belong to all Spaniards as a window into Spain's art.

D. Antonio Izquierdo García

General of the DEM Infantry Brigade

Director of the Army Museum

About painters, history, and battles

For many people the military painter is no more than a draftsman of uniforms, helmets, and feathers, as if there wasn't a human heart beating under the shell of a soldier, as if, by painting him, the man itself would not be painted ...

Leon Plée, Les Annales (The Annals), 1913

For a different perspective, it is a palpable fact that there is a scarcity of pictorial production of military history—regarded as a special department within historic painting—prevalent in Spain in the ninenteenth century compared to other countries. We did not have a Gros nor a Lejeune, nor a Raffet, Vernet, or Charlet, who illustrate with their brushes or lithographies the events during the French Convention (1793–95) or against the Napoleonic invasion of 1808–14. In those times Spain lost many battles due to the absurdity of confronting an enemy superior in equipment, armament, training, and battle experience. Other battles were won—victories that seemed impossible, such as at Bailén, Alcañíz, La Albuera, Vitoria, and San Marcial. That war was won with small actions—ambushes and surprises—which is perhaps why no one bothered to paint them, as they were not appropriate for the large epic canvases that characterized this era. Also, there was not much time left for celebration because, following the war of independence, a long rosary of civilian conflicts on the peninsula as well as overseas ensued.

Leaving aside the ingenious work of Goya, who immortalized the popular insurrection in the streets of Madrid in May 1808, we can only discuss José Aparicio e Inglada, who painted what could be the first exponent of the genre in Spain, his *Batalla de San Marcial* (Battle of San Marcial), in 1821. One would have to fast-forward almost to the mid-nineteenth century to encounter the first painters of Spanish battles: Van Halen and Ricardo Balaca—curiously both foreigners; Sans and Cabot; Casado del Alisal; Fortuny; and somewhat later, the Álvarez-Dumont brothers, Morelli or Cusachs. They immortalized essential occurrences from the Carlist Wars or the African War of 1859. But none of these figures compare in production to the three main painters of military history par excellence of the late nineteenth century: the French Detaille, De Neuville, and Meissonier.

A visit to the Parisian army museum (*Château des Invalides*), the Imperial War Museum in London, or to the Brussels and Warsaw museums allows us to undertake a journey along the centuries of military history of their respective nations via their war and battle paintings. Unfortunately, the same is not true for our Spain as, despite the fact that our museum owns excellent works, their lack is quite apparent. How is it possible that only a few have chosen to recreate episodes of Spain's military history during the full bloom of classicism and romanticism?

Ink drawing by José Cusachs

The impact of the wars that afflicted Spain during the nineteenth century and its permanent confrontation

Frederic Remington, Harpers Magazine, 1897

between liberal and conservative ideology clearly left a deep impact on society. Perhaps then it is difficult to select which patriotic glories to represent in a divided country, so many of them dealt with the war of independence: the last grand occasion when Spaniards united while faced with an invader. Nevertheless, one must point out that there was a sizable production of the African War of 1859, as well as the last of the Carlist Wars, perhaps due to the fact that a part of society that had directly or indirectly been witness demanded it. One can also consider Spain's considerable and chronic indifference towards its own history and, by extension, to the men and women who forged it.

The era of formation of the liberal state presents the apogee of historicist painting, which, through the recreation of the historic events that created the nation of citizens, searched for its iconographic roots. It reaches its culmination with the appearance of European nationalism and does so with the great current tradition, so-called artistic realism. In Spain, despite the state's initiative with the famous *Exposiciones Nacionales de Bellas Artes* (National Fine Arts Exhibits) to foment the genre, works depicting battle scenes that were presented at these exhibits were far and few during the nineteenth century. Among the most well-known is *La rendición de Bailén* (The Rendition of Bailén), by Antonio Gisbert. There are other painters who have left behind outstanding works: Mariano Fortuny and his two large paintings of the African War; Palmarolli and his *Batalla de Tetuán* (Battle of Tetuán); Eduardo Banda y Pineda and his *Carga de Treviño* (Attack at Treviño); and Sans y Cabot and his *Batalla de los Castillejos* (Battle of the Castillejos)—the latter three being kept at the Army Museum. More contemporary artists are the two maestros José Cusachs—a student of Detaille in Paris, who was not exactly prolific at paintings that recreated battle scenes—and Mariano Bertuchi, who specialized in paintings set in the Protectorate of Morocco.

During the turn of the century, the colonial disaster in Spain coincides with a change of political interest towards paintings with a societal context. While some intellectuals of the generation of '98—not entirely with a lack of argument—suggested bringing this approach to a close, others saw the painting of battles as an elation of bellicose sentiment, and even a provocation for war. In France, Meissonier and Detaille suffered ferocious attacks from a sector of art critics who labeled their work patriotizing and heaped ridicule on their attention to detail. However, others wrote:

> *The lectures of dignity, disinterested sacrifice, useful devotion unknown to us which they present, they bring honor to an artist much more than by the mere elation of the form and culture, sometimes egotistical and sterile by their sheer beauty ...*

A short time later, the slaughter of the war from 1914 to 1918 and the defeat of 1940 brought an end to the general public's appreciation for war paintings in France. In Spain, echoes of the long campaigns in Morocco and decades of social upheaval also brought the death of the genre, whose last exponent might well be *Desembarco de Alhucemas* (Landing at Alhucemas) by Moreno Carbonero, painted in 1928. If the first third of the twentieth century brought a generalized lack of interest in historicist painting, another round occurred in the last third, when grand historic canvases remained forgotten in the warehouses of many museums, without any consideration by art historians. It is interesting to note that in 1967, a certain Salvador Dalí organized a homage to no less than Meissonier at the *Hôtel Meurice* in Paris. At this occasion Dalí admitted his admiration for painters of battle scenes:

> *[They] have assimilated the history of our times with regards to its complexity, density, inevitability, tragedy ... regardless of the accepted principles which result from the myopic contemporary aesthetic, Detaille will soon be classified as the superior painter of the living structures of the future while Cézanne will be the one painting the decrepit structures of the past ...*

In Spain this caused the relocation of some artworks and the deterioration of conservation of others. As such, very notable works like *El gran día de Gerona* (The Great Day of Verona) by Álvarez Dumont suffered grave deterioration, while *Batalla de San Marcial* (Battle of San Marcial) by José Aparicio was completely destroyed—perhaps the most sensitive and unfortunate loss, as it was the first of the genre. But the worst result was the state of dispersion in which many of these pieces are found today. For example, *Muerte de Churruca en Trafalgar* (Churruca's Death at Trafalgar) is located in an institute on the Canary Islands, *Rocroi* by Morelli is in a museum in Santander, and the *Episodio de la batalla de Bailén* (Episode of the Battle of Bailén) by Balaca is in a forgotten office of the Ministry of Justice. Only the recent expansion of the *Museo Nacional del Prado* and the efforts of a few restorers have once again made it possible to appreciate such important works as *Fusilamiento de Torrijos* (Execution of Torrijos) by Gisbert, a work commissioned to feature the sacrifice of the liberals during the first third of the nineteenth century.

Will it be possible in the future to see all of the battle paintings in one place, ideally at the Army Museum? Our museum's collection features a notable gallery of personal portraits of all the epochs. Nevertheless, the same cannot be said for battle paintings. It has always been difficult to incorporate new pieces into the musuem's collection, and the larger part of the existing ones was acquired through donations or endowments. The aforementioned scarcity of paintings is also due to budgetary limitations that left many works the museum would have liked to acquire in private hands.

It is patently obvious that today some countries are experiencing a renovated interest in battle paintings. The last years of the twentieth century brought with them a new interest in the topic when rich collectors such as the American Forbes began purchasing works by Detaille and Meissonier to the astonishment of a market keen on avant garde. Figurative art represents shapes and forms, with tendencies toward procuring its verisimilitude (artistic realism). Modern currents of figurative art, realism, and hyperrealism have opened opportunities for a group of painters who reflect historic episodes on their canvases with utmost precision. The weapons, equipment, uniforms, and authentically represented flags completely reflect those utilized during the era and each painting becomes a profound object of historical investigation.

In the US, several artists have successfully dedicated themselves to this genre, not only because of their private clients, but because of commissions from museums and institutions. As to Europe, one can best refer to a group of illustrators of historical military art—the most well-known ones—from France and England, although there are those from other countries as well, at the center and north of the continent.

And Spain? There is indeed a handful of magnificent illustrators that we also count with one or the other painter who works in this genre. And we should point out that we are fortunate to have Augusto Ferrer-Dalmau, who is currently one of the best battle painters in the world, among them.

Execution of Torrijos, by A. Gisbert, courtesy of the Alcoyana Unión de Seguros

Augusto Ferrer-Dalmau Nieto was born on January 20, 1964, in Barcelona. From early childhood he lived with a passion for painting thanks to his mother, María Francisca Nieto Fernández. On many occasions he could contemplate at his house the canvases of military subjects of the Moroccan Wars painted by his mother. The daughter of a cavalry military man, she had spent her childhood and adolescence immersed in a society that revolved around the army of the Spanish Protectorate of Morocco, between the cities Larache and Tetuán. On various occasions Dalmau admitted it was his

mother who had inspired his passion for military subjects. It would be she who would give him his first lectures about Spain's military history and decisively influence and stoke his appreciation and interest that the artist has felt for Spanish military affairs throughout his entire life. To perfect his technique he took part in the famous *Escuela libre del mediterráneo* (Free Mediterranean School) of the great Barcelona painter Torrens Lladó at calle Diputació 329, where students from all over the world assist. It is likely he came to know the magnificent and original style that represented the grand European pictoric tradition. At seventeen he applied to the army's recruitment center and later did military service in Pamplona in 1984—a period he fondly remembers. Towards the end of the 1980s he worked as a textile designer for various top companies around Barcelona and Malaga, but he always kept his passion for oil painting alive. His passion for military matters also brought him from an early age to the world of miniature soldiers, and to paint military figures with acrylic paint or with watercolors, which he later gave away to friends. His first independent works were landscapes, particularly marinas. Later he was inspired by the works of Antonio López and focused on urban landscapes and scenes, capturing the corners of his native town on canvases in a masterful way. His first exhibit would occur in Alicante and later at the Urgel Gallery in Barcelona. There would be many more, and he received accolades and favorable criticism, as well as exhibitions selling out completely. From then on he entered the world market for merchants of art. The works of that period are collected in a monograph by the author and in several books of contemporary art.

In the last decade of the twentieth century he decided to wholly dedicate himself to historic military pieces and started producing canvases with detailed landscapes interlaced with soldiers and horses. In 2002, he had his first successful thematic exhibit of the Carlist Wars at the Arcadia Gallery in Madrid. This was followed by annual exhibitions in the Spanish captial, as well as in New York, France, and England.

Having settled in Valladolid a few years ago, he has collaborated with several publishers, associations, and entities specializing in the diffusion of Spain's military history. He is a particularly assiduous collaborator with the army, its Institute of Military History and Culture, and with the Ministry of Defense, with which he has participated in various recent exhibitions. He is currently one of Spain's most outstanding realist painters and a noted expert on paintings of military subjects. He is also highly regarded by our soldiers and has the acknowledgment of many aficionados of military history, both in Spain as well as abroad, where his work is starting to become known and disseminated.

Augusto Ferrer-Dalmau has said that among his references are the classics of Meissonier, Detaille, and Cusachs, as well as the original works of American Fréderic Remington, who specialized in portraits of the American cavalry during the campaigns against the Indians. They also include the British Lady Butler and, above all, Caton Woodville, and in particular the Frenchman Alphonse de Neuville, an author dedicated to what has been called "the epic of defeat." Just as in the works of the French painter, Dalmau's work exudes an intense and dramatic patriotism. His compositions and figures are full of life and transmit the emotion of the things they have lived through without hiding the misery and suffering inherent in war and falling for facile sensationalism. His mastery of composition, light, landscape, and the movement of horses and men is supreme. The secret is very simple, according to his own words:

> *Everybody has a talent, but most do not develop it. When you do, it is like someone playing by ear but practicing a lot. When you have this gift you work it for hours and hours and days and nights, and it is rare to not reach the mastery of the matter ...*

Ferrer-Dalmau has given us the immense, albeit ethereal, satisfaction to be able to contemplate episodes of Spanish history that we thought we would not be able to see recreated on his canvas: the soldiers of the eighteenth century of the new Bourbon Army in action during the war of Spanish succession or the battles in Africa; the attack of the zapadores of Alcalá rebelling against the orders of the African-French authorities to join them in the fight against the invaders; the charges of the cavalry during the war of 1859 or during the Cuban campaign; the solitary heroism of captain Arenas Gaspar facing Monte Arruit; and the regulars of Morocco or the components of the Spanish voluntary division in Russia. And still those he can gift to our eyes: other forgotten battles during the war of independence, faraway overseas theaters of war, the Spanish civil war, and so many others. Dalmau contributes to our history coming alive, assimilating the grand tradition of European realism and a long list of Catalonian figurative painters who dedicated themselves to painting the history of Spain, providing it with a personal and modern touch. In Dalmau's work we will not find the elation of violence, nor patriotism or gratuitous effects, but we will encounter parts of virtues and realities that are part of extreme situations: the comradeship between members of a regiment that alone makes it possible for a group of men to put their duty in front of their individuality; the grandiose solitude of a sentinel at dawn; and the abnegation and the altruism, determination, and sacrifice for a few ideals. These concepts may sound strange to many, but other people practice them every day, not only in theaters of war, but in contemporary peace, where many social needs are very pressing.

Just for the sake of it, us aficionados feel pure pleasure towards history when we see a homage to those who in the past have sacrificed themselves for the collective—those principles that someone has called the "banners of our fathers"—it is of great value to be able to count among us a painter such as Augusto, whose works will one day be displayed in Spanish military museums, filling a vacuum that Spain's artists of the nineteenth century could not entirely fill.

José Manuel Guerrero Acosta

Commissioner of the exhibition *Augusto Ferrer-Dalmau, art, history and miniatures*

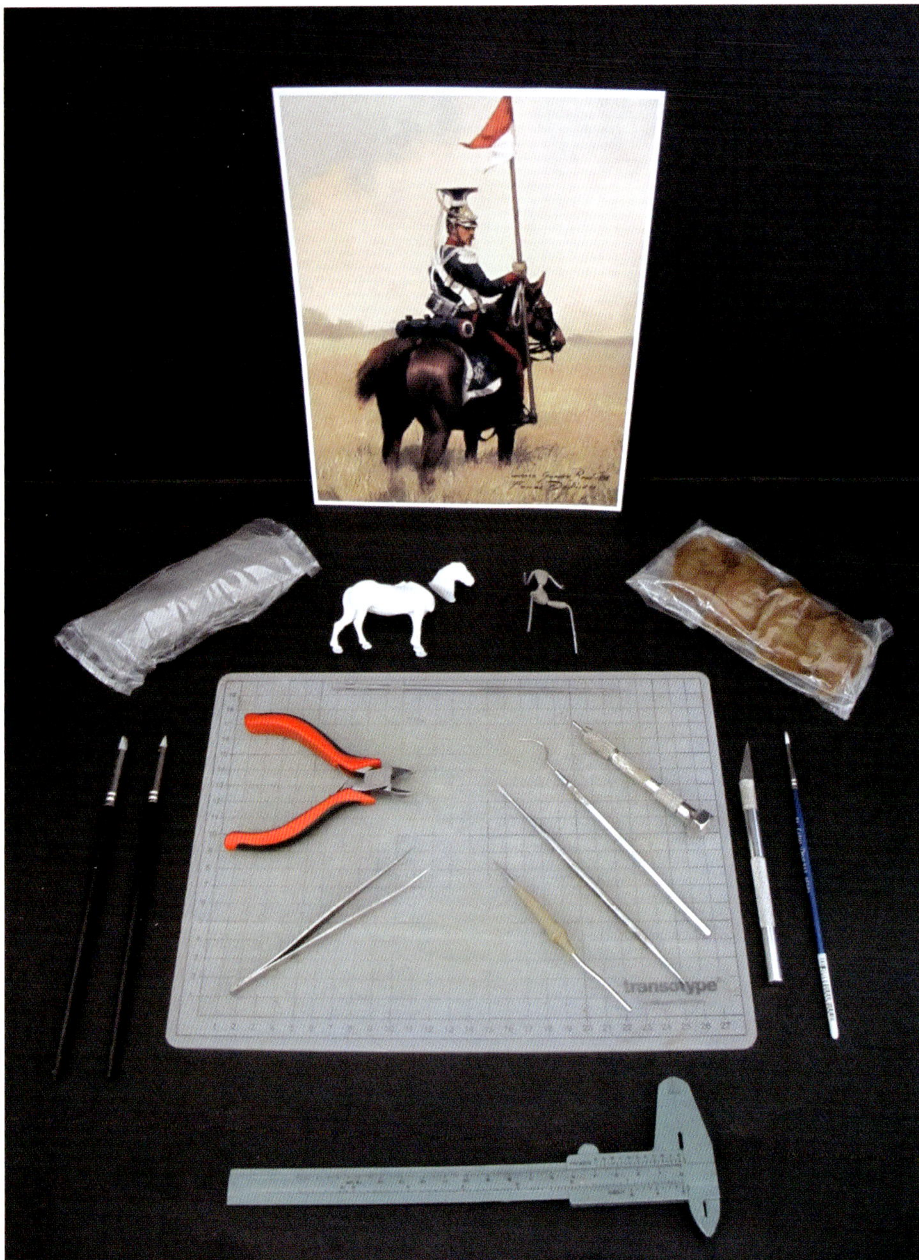

Sculpting and painting military miniatures

The making of small figures with military characteristics being understood as an artistic object, child's toy, or ethnic reference goes back to the origin of civilization. The miniature warriors made from painted wood that were found in the tomb of a prince of the eleventh Egyptian dynasty and are now shown at the Cairo Museum constitute one example. There are also small soldiers made from ceramics, bronze, or lead found during Greek and Roman excavations exhibited at the British Museum and, closer to Spain, the figures that were discovered in the sanctuaries and necropolises of the Iberian peninsula.

Although usually scale reproduction of soldiers has been synonymous with toys, with an emphasis on military formations as opposed to the representation of isolated individuals, sculptural work of this kind has been routinely applied to making prototypes as a prior step to monumental sculpture, with the manufacture of bas-reliefs and medals, or simply because of the enjoyment of sculpting in a more accessible and practical format than that of large urban sculptures. From the great Leonardo da Vinci and Benvenuto Cellini to our "more modest" national sculptors like Mariano Benlliure, Ulpiano Checa, and Sergio Blanco, all have touched upon the small historical or military sculpture over the course of their work.

Despite obvious differences, the common nexus between these sculptures and the traditional "little lead soldier" (including figures the reader will discover in this book) goes back to the last quarter of the twentieth century when, for safety reasons, the production and sale of metal figures as toys for children was prohibited, as their production involved the use of materials that might be hazardous to their health. We can say that at this moment the military miniature was born as such: a hobby for adults where professional artisans offer miniature soldiers to the aficionado made from metal or resin and sold as single pieces or in kits that are prepared, mounted, and painted with a personalized touch added by the hobbyist's skill and experience. Later on, some of the very same aficionados developed their own sculptural abilities and designs and manufactured their own figures.

Today, the number of modelers who make their own works is increasing in a craft that combines classical sculpture, model construction, historical investigation, and artistic painting. The result is a unique piece that might be destined either for production and sale or for private or personal collections. At any rate, the level of realism of many military miniatures made today is quite surprising and perfectly comparable to the small sculptures of the distinguished artists mentioned earlier. To avoid incorrect interpretations, we are not affirming that military miniaturism represents an art; not because of a lack of intrinsic value, but due to common sense, as this activity is still laden with limitations that prevent such consideration, particularly today, when artistic definitions are taking other routes.

Some ideas and manufacturers in this field approach and connect with certain concepts, which, although they may turn out to be classic, succeed at providing life and creating a communicative piece capable of transmitting a message. They allow spectators to participate in the artistic game, awakening their capacity of interpretation, something very basic, and closing the circle of the artistic process creator-artwork-spectator.

Generally speaking, small-format sculptures or miniatures do not vary a lot from the technique utilized for large-scale objects. Irrespective of its size, if the artwork has been obtained traditionally by sculpting directly in marble, stone, or wood, or modeled in clay, playa dough, or plaster—with the following mold made from bronze, stone, etc.—the material mostly used today by modelers is epoxy resin consisting of two components that, when mixed in equal parts, start to become hard. The resulting piece has good properties once dry: it can be drilled, ground, and shaped. The use of different materials to shape this resin is an essential element and very personal, usually involving scalpels, rubber and hair brushes, needles, and blades.

The process of making a human figure depends on the personal technique of the modeler, but it usually starts with making a wire frame skeleton that will determine the pose and anatomical measurements. Small applications of resin on this frame make up the muscles and provide a rough shape to the limbs, torso, and head. Once the piece is dry the anatomy is "dressed" from bottom to top, overlapping garments and thereby creating the precise volume. The final step is to create the facial expression together with the selected body language to give it its intended look.

If the intention of the modeler is to create a unique piece, the process of sculpturing terminates here. If the idea is to make copies then the process of cloning and editing the piece will take place with the use of molds, just as with sculptural art. Different techniques for reproduction can be chosen according to the desired final result: reductions, baking pieces, preparation of waxes or resins for casting, the application of metal, etc.

Nevertheless, the basics of military miniatures do not end with the modeling of the piece or the casting of it, which is the last step in classic sculpture. The process ends with the decoration of the figure.

Painting each miniature requires prior planning, with the point of departure a detailed study of the historical subject in question and each of the physical details that the modeling intends to portray. The connection to reality is provided by its decoration, as the paint provides the figure with new aspects and looks that the sculpture by itself cannot really convey.

The painting of figures has advanced just like proper military miniatures themselves, trying to outdo each other with each piece and always in search of the most extreme realism, while at the same time providing the precise artistic connotation that converts each piece into something unique and of high quality.

The materials used depend on the painter and his or her preferences, as the current marketplace offers a veritable universe of products for visual artists. Although it is true that among Spanish modelers acrylic paint is the most common technique and one which they have pioneered, there are more and more artisans who are switching to oil paint, enamel, or mixed techniques. The attitude that one should work with whichever paint is comfortable is increasingly common. With this kind of activity it is not the utilized material that converts a modeler into a great artist or sculptor but the way it is utilized. In this respect the pigment is only one more tool.

Other issues are more relevant, such as control of the paint itself, the type of illumination, or the quest for expressiveness through color. When combined well, all these aspects provide the piece with its unique and personal character.

The collection of miniatures in this catalog is the result of adapting the visual work of Augusto Ferrer-Dalmau to a three-dimensional space, trying to capture his particular vision of the different historical moments he portrayed and applying his own technique as to color, lighting from above, and the position of the objects. Ferrer-Dalmau's merit is to have brought to life the texts and descriptions of battles, gestures, and moments of military life, where each painting tells a story he himself has recreated. Dramatization, compassion, pride, and solitude are characteristics present in each image. The miniaturist only had to copy the artist's imprint, leaving the rest to technique. Nevertheless, the challenge was considerable, as bringing volume to a painting of two dimensions is not without difficulty. Imagining spaces, creating subjects that can only be guessed from the canvas, and investigating the invisible areas of characters, flags, and other objects requires work and effort.

Although these miniatures are not the best examples of an author's creativity in military miniatures, they are indeed a tribute by a small group to the work of an admired painter. His appearance on the Spanish art scene with his purely military paintings has created an authentic revolution among miniaturists who have been inspired by his very first paintings.

Finally, the images that accompany this text and serve to show the modeling and painting of a miniature figure correspond to the work titled *Lancero trigalero* (Lancer in Wheatfield), based on the canvas by Augusto Ferrer-Dalmau of the same name. The horseman—a lancer of the Royal Guard of Fernando VII—was modeled by Antonio Zapatero Guardini while the painting was done by Jesús Gamarra López. Both miniaturists have captured the placid quietness of the soldier and horse in the wheat field and the calm attitude towards any sign of alarm, playing with the color of the uniform, which the sun's rays intensify. The detail of the wheat ears provides more realism to the scene, if that is possible.

Although unknown to the vast majority, military miniatures have the capacity of surprising those who look at them and usually create a sensation of admiration for the precision and perfection that these small pieces and objects embody.

As a participant of this tribute in miniatures I hope you will appreciate what you see here.

Luis Miguel Esteban Laguardia

Miniaturist

Spain's military history through miniatures and the paintings of Ferrer-Dalmau

If the individualism that characterizes the Spanish people is a distinguishing moral trait that is part of our cultural idiosyncrasy, then in the case of the introverted world of military miniatures this trait at times reaches extreme levels. Nevertheless, at certain moments and with adequate incentive we manage to come together to reach a common objective, giving our very best and succeeding in converting this individuality, which might be considered a defect, into a virtue. As such, and increasingly more frequently, there are cultural miniaturist associations where part of its members join efforts to realize joint projects of extraordinary quality. However, in order to unite miniaturists from the four cardinal points of the Iberian peninsula in one single project such as the present one some special motivation is necessary.

On two former occasions a group of Spanish miniaturists came together as one to pay homage through their individual or collective works to two eminent artists who had dedicated most of their artistic work to military history: the exhibitions based on the work of Catalonian painter José Cusachs y Cusachs and the illustrator Dionisio Álvarez Cueto from León. The exhibitions took place while taking advantage of celebrations of international miniaturist competitions: in the case of Cusachs, the Miniaturism World Championship in Gerona in 2008; in the case of Dionisio Álvarez, a competition that took place in the city of Toledo at the beginning of June 2010. The thirty or so miniatures seen in Gerona grew to some fifty in Toledo, proving the increasing interest of the participants in these projects. Hence, after the success of the two mentioned exhibits us miniaturists are coming together once again, not only to show our works outside of the microcosm of competitions and regular contests, but to pay tribute and bring attention to the work of a historical military painter who has done the most to promote the military life of Spain over the course of its history. I am referring to Barcelona painter Augusto Ferrer-Dalmau Nieto. Someone whose oil paintings serve as an inexhaustible fountain of inspiration and who shares with us the complicity that his dedication to miniatures from a young age has given him. In this present opportunity, taking advantage of the incomparable setting offered by the Army Museum of the city of Toledo, sixty-three miniaturists and associations from Spain and Portugal have come together to give life to sixty-two original artworks based on the canvases of the Catalonian artist; sixty-two works that reproduce scenes and personalities of Spanish military history over the course of four centuries. In addition, the presence of the works of the artist paid homage to was unavoidable. After a major organizational effort and a total commitment by Augusto Ferrer-Dalmau, almost twenty original canvases were gathered, plus over fifty high-quality reproductions of his oil paintings and eight sketches created *ex profeso* for the occasion.

Although the number of works is significant, this is not about an exhibit where canvases and miniatures are mixed together and the number of exhibits is primary and above any other consideration. The main aspect is that the exhibit may turn into a message expressed in visual terms that supports the contact and communication between the figure and the visitor. For this to be possible, adequate museographical tools have to be utilized to achieve the desired goal. Ultimately, the idea is to tell a story in the most orderly and didactic manner, just as is the case with any temporary or permanent museum exhibit. In this case the purpose is to show part of Spain's history via a chronological itinerary that aids the spectator admiring the reconstructions of the past via two art disciplines: painting and miniatures.

It might be somewhat pretentious to consider miniatures as one more tangible artistic expression, keeping in mind this opinion is not shared by a large part of the general public, nor by the majority of experts or critics of the art world, who classify them as mere handicraft and toys. Even among miniaturists themselves, whether professionals or not, opinions regarding this matter are divergent.

I could try to justify my statement by quoting the cold and concise words of the Royal Academy of the Spanish Language. One of its definitions of art is any human activity that expresses a personal vision of either the real or imaginary via materials, language, or sound. The same dictionary defines miniatures as an artistic object of small scale. However, the definition of art encompasses a large number of aspects and particular considerations that are very much influenced by subjective opinion. Ultimately there is no possible objective explanation, however, I consider the best option is that we let the spectator look at each of the miniatures and decide whether they are capable of transmitting a stream of sensations and emotions that one can enjoy. If they do then small sculptures that are magnificently painted might be acknowledged as authentic pieces of art. Augusto Ferrer-Dalmau thought about this matter and expressed it in these words: "I am an unconditional supporter of miniaturism; it is a genuine artistic expression just like sculpture or painting. It should be part of the gallery circuit, and actually in Spain there are projects for exhibits of the highest level that I am honored to participate in, where the degree of sophistication and perfection is reaching incredible heights that were impossible only a few years ago..."

The pieces that are part of this exhibit show more than three hundred years of Spanish military history. The selection will provide the spectator with a unique cultural voyage, starting with the battlefields of the Thirty Year War and featuring the majority of the military and political conflicts that involved Spanish troops, ending with the immense and freezing Russian steppes during World War II. A selection that allows us to contemplate historic battles, portraits of celebrated personalities, glorious cavalry charges, desperate combat, heroic actions, precious landscape and urban scenes with a romantic touch, bucolic canvases showing daily life and the interaction of the militia and civilians, and even the allegoric wink of an eye to one of the most relevant characters of world literature: Don Quijote de la Mancha. A collection that also shows us the evolution of uniforms and equipment of the Spanish armies over the course of the centuries, each constituting an authentic sketch of history.

With respect to the small sculptures and the not-so-small ones, most of them (about 65%) are modeled on a scale of 54 mm[1], which is the king scale for this type of model because of its excellent relation between size and the details shown. However, other sizes and categories are also represented. We can admire impressive dioramas with close to seventy figures on a scale of 28 mm; large-scale models close to 300 mm, where the level of detail and realism is absolutely incredible; spectacular mounted soldiers up to 90 mm high; busts; and even flat and semi-relief figures. The following—taking advantage of the different historic periods to which the pieces have been cataloged—will briefly make reference to them and point out a few of them that we believe merit it in this introduction because of their singularity, complexity, or size. Actually, to be honest, they all have merit, but the four pages I have been provided with as the framework of this introduction would turn into several dozen.

Hence, *"Rocroi," el último tercio* ("Rocroi," the Last Third)—one of the most impressive canvases Augusto Ferrer-Dalmau has painted so far—initiates the journey through history. The canvas brazenly portrays the final moments of the Battle of Rocroi (1643), with particular protagonism given to the sentiments and states of mind of the figures who compose the scene. These very figures have inspired no less than four miniatures representing the five most emblematic ones. The period of the Thirty Year War is closed with a vignette titled *Alférez de España* (Spanish Second Lieutenant), which because of its extraordinary quality has been awarded the Army's Award in the category of dioramas or vignettes in the 2012 edition. We now change centuries and enter the era preferred by Augusto Ferrer-Dalmau, where the colorful and spectacular uniforms of the nineteenth century are a continuous source of inspiration; a predilection that explains why most of his work is set in this epoch. There are forty-two pieces associated with the nineteenth century. The historic route begins with the war of independence (1808–1814), a conflict whose bicentennial anniversary is still celebrated with the inauguration of exhibits, historical events, and the publication of a large number of books and articles. In our case there are seven paintings and eight miniatures (two of which have used the same canvas as the

1 To identify the scale of miniature figures the distance in millimeters (mm) from the feet to the eyes of the figure is measured.

model) to remind us of those ill-fated days. Despite the fact that all of the sculptures are exceptional, the diorama *La Batalla de Bailén* ("The Battle of Bailén"), with its seventeen figures at a scale of 54 mm, has to be pointed out because of its difficulty and the enormous work involved, as well as the applied concept for the pieces, where natural materials such as fabrics, leathers, wood, or sheet metal, among others, have been utilized. One must point out the exceptional lancer based on one of the protagonists of the oil painting *Lanceros de la Legión Extremeña* ("Lancers of the Extremadura Legion"), which because of its size and realism seems to have jumped out of the canvas, wanting to talk to us.

The First Carlist War (1833–1840) frames eighteen figures and scenes, where we would point out a lancer of the Royal Guard (*Lancero trigalero*, "Lancer in Wheat Field"), which serves as an example to explain the complete process of modeling and painting of these miniatures to the general public. We continue with two mounted figures set in the era of the Second Carlist War (1846–1849) to get to a group of four works set in the second half of the century. Here two pieces featuring the *Guardia Civil* (Civil Guard)—an institution created in 1844—have been included; a spectacular equestrian sculpture made at a 90-mm scale based on one of Augusto Ferrer-Dalmau's favorite units: the Princess' Hussars; and finally, the aforementioned reminiscence of Don Quijote and his faithful squire Sancho Panza, with the famous nobleman wearing a Carlist uniform.

With respect to the campaigns in North Africa during the middle of the century, we stop at a famous battle that occurred in 1848 in the area of Melilla, where deputy sergeant Ignacio Fernández of the Numancia Regiment—after his horse is killed by a bullet—gets up and attacks the enemy with sword in hand shouting "Where my horse dies, so do I." The episode has been immortalized in a magnificent canvas and by a group of sculptors whose quality merited the award for best work of the Sixth Miniaturist Convention *San Lorenzo del Escorial*, July 2012.

The nineteenth century concludes with three works featuring the last Carlist War (1872–1876) and a magnificent scene showing one of the Spanish cavalry charges of the last of the Cuban Wars (1895–1898), with the horsemen wearing the characteristic uniform with ultramarine stripes.

Now fully within the twentieth century, sixteen original works show us the precious uniforms of Alfonso XIII and go once again to the north of Morocco, where the Campaign of Melilla of 1909 and the disaster of Annual in 1921 are remembered with several sculptures of outstanding quality. A bold diorama with three mounted figures representing one of the most incredible and heroic charges of the entire history of the Spanish cavalry must be pointed out here: the one that occurred on September 20, 1909, to the north of Melilla, close to the town of Taxdirt, where sixty-five men of the Fourth Squadron of Alfonso XII charged against a mass of about one thousand five hundred Riffean enemies.

The last Civil War (1936–1939), with one single figure representing the legionnaires in front of Madrid University, precedes the last historical period of this exhibition: World War II. A conflict where a division of Spanish volunteers, the so-called Blue Division, participated together with the German Army fighting Soviet troops. The event was recorded via two dioramas of 54 mm and two impressive figures, which, because of their quality, technique, and size, will surprise the viewer.

Finally, allow me to give you a recommendation: spend a few minutes observing each painting and miniature in detail; enjoy the poses and expressions of the protagonists, the magnificent horses, the eye-catching garments, and the multitude of small details that will undoubtedly surprise you; allow yourself to be guided by this group of artists through this time tunnel you have in front of you, and you will find out that the journey was worthwhile.

Please, enjoy.

Agustín Pacheco Fernández

Miniaturist and member of the Institute of History and Military Culture

GALLERY OF PAINTINGS AND MINIATURES

Bust
Pablo Ronda and Eduardo Sánchez

Bust
Pablo Ronda and Eduardo Sánchez

Details of the painting
"Rocroi" *El último tercio*
("The Last Third")

"Rocroi" *El último tercio*
("The Last Third")

Flat figure
Rafael Cebrián

Figure
Diego Fortes & Fernando Ruiz

Details of the painting "Rocroi" *El último tercio* ("The Last Third")

Vignette
Luis Angel Ruiz

Alférez de los Tercios españoles 1640 ("Second Lieutenant of the Spanish Third")

Figure
Antonio Meseguer and
Samuel Pérez

La gesta de los zapadores ("The Feat of the Sappers")

Diorama
Jesús Gamarra

Bailén

Figure
Albert Gros

Toma de Gerona ("Capture of Gerona")

Vignette
Joan Masferrer

La guerra de mossén Rovira ("The War of Mossén Rovira")

Lancero de Sevilla ("Lancer of Seville")

Vignette
Patxi Vacas

Lanceros de la Legión Extremeña
("Lancers of the Extremadura Legion")

Figure
Miguel Angel Díaz Galeote

Detail of the painting *Lanceros de la Legión Extremeña* ("Lancers of the Extremadura Legion")

Mounted figure
Rafael Gil

Coracero 1811
("Cuirassier")

Bust
Antonio Meseguer and
Francisco Javier Ruiz

Trompeta de húsares
("Hussar Trumpet")

Mounted figure
Antonio Zapatero and
Jesús Gamarra

Lancero de la Guardia Real, 1835
("Lancer of the Royal Guard")

Flat figures
Antonio Zapatero and
Juan Francisco Estevez

Guardias Reales en el cielo
("Royal Guards in Heaven")

Vignette
Francisco Javier Ruiz and
Luis Sanz

La Guardia Real en campaña
("The Royal Guard during a campaign")

Vignette
Iñigo Rodríguez and
Julio Cabos

Húsares de la Princesa, 1836
("Princess' Hussars")

Mounted figure
Jesús Gamarra

General Diego de León

Diorama
Alberto Fernández

La Cincomarzada
("The Cincomarzada")

Vignette
Antonio Meseguer and
José Hernández

La madre
("The Mother")

Diorama
Asociación Alabarda (Alabarda Association)
(Antonio Zapatero , Angel Aparicio, Francisco Javier Ruiz,
Alejandro Labourdette, Fernando Pérez, Manuel Iglesias,
Juan Fco. Estevez, Miguel Angel Pérez)

Calderote ("Calderote")

Lancero de Doña Margarita
("Doña Margarita Lancer")

Flat figure
Rafael Cebrián

Escuadrón de Navarra
("Navarra Squadron")

Vignette
Rafael Torres, Luis Miguel Garcia, Luis García,
Alejandro Labourdette, and José Antonio San Martín

Lanceros de Navarra
("Navarra Lancers")

Mounted figure
Waldo Osés and Roberto Ramírez

A por la embestida
("The Charge")

Diorama
Waldo Osés and Gustavo Gil

Carga de Zumalacárregui
("Charge of Zumalacárregui")

Figure
Francisco Javier Ruiz

Húsares de Ontoria
("Ontoria Hussars")

Figure
Waldo Osés and
Patxi Vacas

Oriamendi

Vignette
Jesús Gamarra

El final de la batalla
("Battle's End")

Diorama
Roberto Ramírez, David Hernanz, Isaac Jaramillo, and Miguel Angel Pérez

General Cabrera

Mounted figure
Sergio Reguero

Trote
("Trot")

Mounted figure
Javier Aldabe, Fco. Javier Ruiz, and
Manuel Iglesias

Lancero de Farnesio
("Farnesio Lancer")

Mounted figure
Salvador Ortigosa

Húsar de la Princesa
("Princess' Hussar")

Vignette
Jorge Fernández and
José Manuel García

Pareja de Guardias Civiles
("Pair of Civil Guards")

Mounted figure
Juan Carlos García Benitez

Guardia Civiles a caballo
("Mounted Civil Guards")

Vignette
Miguel Angel Pérez

Quijotada Carlista
("Carlist-style Don Quijote")

Diorama
Waldo Osés and
José Gallardo

Donde muere mi caballo…
("Where My Horse Dies...")

Bust
Albert Gros and
Juan Miguel Fernández

Adelante jinetes del Farnesio!
("Go ahead, Farnesian horsemen!")

Semi-relief figures
Antonio Zapatero and
Miguel Angel Garrido

Cabo y trompeta de húsares 1860
("Corporal and Hussar trumpet")

Mounted figure
Genaro Ortega

Wad Ras. Húsar de la Princesa 1860
("Wad Ras. Princess' Hussar")

Mounted figure
Pablo Ronda and
Eduardo Sánchez

Cazador de Albuera
("Albuera Hunter")

General Savall

Mounted figure
Francisco Morales

Bendiciendo a las tropas
("Blessing the Troops")

Figure
Antonio Zapatero and
Miguel Angel Garrido

El final
("The End")

Diorama
Gregorio Galan and
Gustavo González

Carga de caballería en Cuba, 1897
("Cavalry Charge in Cuba")

Mounted figure
Jordi Gros

Estado mayor 1908
("Greater State")

Mounted figure
Sergio Reguero

Cadetes de caballería
("Cavalry Cadets")

Figure
Ferprad and
Santigo Doel

Húsar de Pavía
("Pavia Hussar")

Mounted figure
Antonio Meseguer and
Cesar de la Peña

Húsar de la Princesa 1909
("Princess' Hussar")

Mounted figure
Waldo Osés and
Roberto Ramírez

Sargento del Rey
("Sargeant del Rey")

Diorama
Luis Esteban Laguardia

La carga de Taxdirt
("The Taxdirt charge")

Mounted figure
Antonio Dafonte

Cabo de la Guardia Civil
("Civil Guard Corporal")

Mounted figure
Antonio Meseguer and
David Lobo

Húsar de Pavía 1921
("Pavia Hussar")

Figure
Antonio Meseguer and
José Hernández

Figure
Jorge Fernández and
Chema García

El capitán Arenas
("Captain Arenas")

Mounted figure
Miguel Angel Pérez and
Agustín Pacheco

Cazador del Alcántara
("Alcántara Hunter")

Figure
Vitalino Chitas

Legión 1936
("Legion")

Figure
Gabriel García Calvo

Voljov. El batallón Román
("Voljov. The Román batallion")

Diorama
Miguel Rojo

Camino a Possad. 1941
("Towards Possad")

Diorama
Jorge Fernández and
Manuel Picatoste

Comandante Barrera, División azul 1941
("Commander Barrera, Blue Division")

Figure
Gabriel García Calvo

Que en Rusia están
("In Russia They Are")

Library of Congress Control Number: 2015954240

ISBN: 978-0-7643-5010-8
Printed in China

Published by Schiffer Publishing, Ltd.
4880 Lower Valley Road
Atglen, PA 19310
Phone: (610) 593-1777; Fax: (610) 593-2002
E-mail: Info@schifferbooks.com
Web: www.schifferbooks.com

For our complete selection of fine books on this and related subjects, please visit our website at www.schifferbooks.com. You may also write for a free catalog.

Schiffer Publishing's titles are available at special discounts for bulk purchases for sales promotions or premiums. Special editions, including personalized covers, corporate imprints, and excerpts, can be created in large quantities for special needs. For more information, contact the publisher.

We are always looking for people to write books on new and related subjects. If you have an idea for a book, please contact us at proposals@schifferbooks.com.